L ⌐

with my

Guardian

Angel

Books by Richard Bach

Life
with my
Guardian
Angel

RICHARD BACH

RAINBOW RIDGE
BOOKS

Cover and interior design by Frame25 Productions
Cover photographs © Lotus_studio c/o Shutterstock.com
and Sergey Nivens c/o Shutterstock.com

Published by:
Rainbow Ridge Books, LLC
140 Rainbow Ridge Road
Faber, Virginia 22938

If you are unable to order this book from your local book-seller, you may order directly from the distributor.

Square One Publishers, Inc.
115 Herricks Road
Garden City Park, NY 11040
Phone: (516) 535-2010
Fax: (516) 535-2014
Toll-free: 877-900-BOOK

Visit the author at: www.richardbach.com

ISBN 978-1-937907-56-3

10 9 8 7 6 5 4 3 2 1

Printed in the United States of America

"He was six years old! And there he was, creeping up on the burro at the ranch . . ."

"Oh, no. 'The burro . . .' That's Pete? Little Dickie was going to try a ride on Pete? The wildest, the wickedest . . . And you just watched?"

"I was in Guardian Angel training," she said. "I suggested to Pete, '*Don't let him get you! Run clear across the corral!*'

"He didn't listen. And I couldn't talk to Dickie . . . everything was happening so fast, and no I didn't think about changing the belief of time . . . I was a little frightened. It was going to be a train wreck!"

"You're sure it was Pete?"

"He didn't care. Anybody who got on his back, he was going to pitch them off."

"And you thought the kid would be killed?"

"Could have happened. Happens all the time. Kids play with live wires, they fall into pools before they learn about swimming, they mess with touchy animals in the desert . . .

there's rocks everywhere, kids get killed every day! You know this one, don't you? He had a destiny . . ."

"Everybody's got a destiny."

"Well, he was my destiny, too, and I didn't want him getting killed at six years old. What kind of guardian angel am I . . . I let my mortal . . . he had agreed to live a long life this time, he had things to say, and next thing he did . . . he hopped up on a wild burro and two seconds later he's flying through the air, comes down on a rock and dies. Then he comes back to heaven and he reminds me that I agreed to be his *guardian angel*, not the Grim Reaper! He asks what happened to me, what happened to his guardian angel, was she having lunch just then?"

"Oh. The crash is his fault, and he blames you?"

"He was six! His mind was all cotton. And now I think I had a few powers that I could have used . . ."

"You got the burro to faint."

"I didn't think of that. Except that Pete was not a good fainter."

"But you knew what was going to happen. Pete was going to pitch your mortal, pitch little Dickie through the air."

"In his own mind Dickie was trying to get higher. That was his first idea of heaven, being higher than anything around. So while Dickie was climbing on Pete's back, the burro was quiet, solemn . . . *'Don't humans know that nobody stays on my back? The little kid just wants to fly through the air for a while, and I'm glad that I can help his wish to come true.'*"

"And you did nothing."

"You see the scene, don't you? The desert, the rocks everywhere, the cactus right near the one patch of sand nearby. I thought to Pete, *go three steps ahead, then pitch him!* And after not much reflecting, that's what Pete did. Three steps put him by the cactus, and the sand alongside. Pete was saddle-free, bridle-free, and he pitched Dickie, who weighed about half a bag of oats, right then. Sure enough the kid flew over the cactus and landed in the sand. No rocks. No injury. No trying to ride Pete again."

"So he picked himself up, he thanked you, he went on with his life?"

"Yes and no. He picked himself up, he didn't thank me. He didn't know I was there, didn't know I talked Pete into saving his life. He ran into the house and told his big brother what happened."

"And . . ."

"His brother," she said, "a few minutes later, no one in the family, believed him. Ever."

"But you know that it happened, didn't you?"

"Is that supposed to be our job? We change mortals' lives, and nobody knows what we've done to help them?"

"If you want a lot of praise," the angel said, "if you want *any* praise, ever, then Guardian Angel is not the job you want."

Silence. Both angels, dressed alike in their white robes, and golden sashes, they looked at the sunrise for a time, and then, while their mortals slept, they flew away.

The difference between rescuing
mortals and helping them, is this:
The rescuer does all the work.

—*The Guardian Angels' Handbook
Volume IX: Working With Your Mortal*

Chapter One

IT TOOK ME seventy-some years before I believed in guardian angels.

Every time my angel managed to save my life, I called it lucky coincidence.

I never mentioned getting myself thrown by Pete in Arizona and landing on the one soft spot on the ranch, never wrote that I had been saved by my angel when I nearly got shot in Riverside. Never even knew about angels, let alone that my guardian angel was a female angel.

Yet these remarkable spirits didn't care that we never knew. My angel's job, after The Desert Years, was to guide me during the Experimenting with Explosives part of my young life.

It was planned to be a rocket. I found a foot of steel pipe, screwed a steel cap on one end of the pipe, a small-diameter gas jet on the other, stuffed it with home-made black powder (*Is this a good idea, Dickie? she said. You've read how to make black powder, did you really have to grind up so much of it?*), fastened the rocket to a small four-wheel cart (*Is this rocket-car going to work the way you hope it will, have you thought about any possible problem with your plan?*), and then decided to light the explosive with a white-hot welding rod (*You're going to do this with no gloves, no blast proof helmet, no asbestos coveralls, you're going to ignite it two feet from your head?*) and expected the car to race down the driveway (*without considering that this wheeled thing which you have manufactured is called a "pipe-bomb"?*), and that the igniter (*you*) would be unharmed (*in the explosion which would follow*).

What fun it will be, I thought, to watch my invention work! Fastened to the rocket, the car would go fast, I thought it could hit maybe 20 mph along the wire that kept it straight down my driveway.

All those faulty links in my plan. Thanks to my guardian angel though, my incredible hopes for the rocket-car sort of worked that morning, including her improvised psychic safety equipment.

I remember pushing the glowing welding-rod into my invention, reaching another half-inch for the powder, and then I remember there wa . . . *WHUFF!* . . . a wall of hot, a cloud of smoke with little sparkles in it.

My rocket-car? It disappeared.

One second it was there, the next, gone. Empty space.

I didn't get exploded, I didn't get burned, and all I found when the smoke cleared, was one wheel of the car. Down the driveway, across the street, there was somebody else's house. No broken windows, no flaming crater on their lawn.

Did I thank if not my angel, did I thank my lucky stars, that I had the extraordinary good fortune to survive the Rocket-Car Experiment?

No. Because I was puzzled . . . what happened to my invention? Only now can I imagine that it must have accelerated past Warp Speed, shifted dimensions, crashed into a lawn on an alternate planet. A host of comments in their strange language:

"How did this sooty three-wheel bomb-vehicle appear in our peaceful neighborhood?"

My Ram-Jet Invention was next. I soldered it up from a few steel pipes, fastened some small jets from the interior, filled it with alcohol, and lit it off.

Today I know that ramjets need to come online at a speed of about 400 miles per hour, so they won't work well at 0 miles per hour. The heat from the alcohol melted the solder after a while, and the whole thing was flames lashed to a pivot on my lawn, thanks to Ms. Guardian Angel (who decided not to mention that I could have welded the seams instead of soldering them).

From there it was a fairly easy life for my angel. I didn't much care for the plans that others made, while I was a teenager. Didn't care for motorcycles . . . well, I did want one, but she whispered to my mother, "*Motorcycle for Dick? Not a good idea.*" So motorcycles were out.

Got a '46 Ford, drove to the beach and then skin-dived, without drowning. I did see a lone seagull flying then, wondered why he flew there when all the other seagulls were on a different beach. What a wonder, when I hid between the huge boulders of the Newport-Balboa jetty: the sound of his wings! flying just over my head. I never forgot the sound of those wings.

That was the end of Easy Street for my Guardian Angel. Like Mr. Toad of *The Wind in the Willows*, I had discovered—*Airplanes!*

A coincidence? At first I didn't much care for airplanes, since they were financially out of reach for me. But in my one and only half-year of college, came the course that changed me for life. Name of the course? Archery.

Standing next to me on the archery range was a stranger. We shot some arrows without a word, and then as he was aiming for the target, a little airplane went over the college. Instead of not-caring, he forgot about archery, and he looked at the airplane.

I don't joke with strangers. Yet I knew he cared about what he had seen. There's a reason why he cares, I thought. I didn't know I had secret desires. I merely spoke, by way of being funny with a stranger, "I'll bet that you have a little airplane and you need someone to wash and polish it for you every week for free, and you'll give him a flying lesson every Tuesday."

That was pretty well how I remember that moment. Not being funny, I think now, it was telling a dream I didn't know, to a stranger I had never met.

He looked at me puzzled, and after a minute he said, "How did you know?" My angel pressed her hand over her mouth so I wouldn't hear her laugh.

I don't remember what I said. Had I known that his words had just changed my life, had I known that my new flight-instructor-to-be had shifted everything that would happen to me in this lifetime, I would have fainted like a burro.

Instead, I drove in my car to Fullerton airport, met his 1946 Luscombe 8E, washed it, polished it every week, and every Tuesday I took my 50-minute flying lesson. Why? My new friend had just become a brand new flight instructor, and he needed a student to practice on.

I always loved heaven. From the first flight with my new friend, I loved flying, too. Also, I was terrified. Spins, mostly, and there was so much to learn! How could I learn it all?

"You'll never learn it all," he said. "Nobody has learned everything about flying and they never will. But if you practice, you can learn enough to be a good pilot, even if you don't know everything."

That was it. I quit school. Takes too long, college. I went to the Navy. "I've always wanted to be a Navy pilot," I told the recruiter. "How do I start?"

"You take some tests, son," said the chief petty officer. "And then you take some training at Pensacola, and you'll be the pilot you're meant to be."

The bright red warning light startled my guardian angel. *"Dick's gonna get killed. I cannot let him join the Navy!"*

She was instantly aware of what would happen, and by now she had the skills to stop terrible things from happening.

An aircraft carrier is a very small place on which to land an airplane. Aircraft carrier crews ask a question to civilians: "Does anyone want a new jet fighter, for free?"

"Yes!" say the civilians, "I want a new jet fighter for free!"

"Good!" they're told. "Just follow an aircraft carrier for a day, and bring a big raft behind you."

The petty officer didn't tell me that. I did as he told me about the tests, and for some reason I couldn't pass the eye test. "Something's wrong," I said. "Can I take this test again?"

"Sure you can."

I tried again, failed again.

Finished with the Navy, I crossed the street to the Air Force recruiter. "Hi," I said to the master sergeant. "I've always wanted to be a Air Force pilot. How do I start?"

"There's a test first, and then you're off to begin flying in Texas, at Lackland Air Base!"

I did as I was told, and passed the eye test. The same test that the Navy gave me.

I passed the eye test thanks to my guardian angel. Flying seemed a good thing to her, since Air Force pilots land on a ten-thousand-foot strip of hard-surface runway, their bases don't float away as soon as they take off, and Air Force pilots have a nice place to sleep.

Passing the test just then, I would have laughed at that. Yet a few years later, crossing the Mediterranean Sea at 36,000 feet in a flight of four Air Force F-84Fs, I saw a little tiny aircraft carrier way down beneath us, floating at the bottom of the sky.

Navy pilots land there, I thought. They go up in terrible weather, they come back in a storm, the carrier deck is thrashing up, down, swerving left and right, the visibility is few hundred yards and they have to put the airplane's tailhook on the number two arresting wire and if anything's wrong with their approach one chance out of two they'll fall off the deck into the black ocean and nobody will see them again.

A few months later, when I had the chance, I asked a carrier pilot, "What's it like, on deck?"

"There's a thousand reasons why a landing can not quite work out," he said. "Wheels come off, rockets jar loose, a landing airplane hits another airplane on deck and they both explode in flames, a cart rolls onto the runway just when an aircraft touches down, the deck makes a sudden change at the last second. When your landing's over, you come back to your little bunk in a steel room shared with seven other guys, and you wonder why you didn't join the Air Force."

When I landed later that day on my two-mile runway, deployed a drag chute to slow down, taxied to a place where nothing moves, even in a storm, I was happy to say that I was not the best pilot in the world. The best pilots are the carrier pilots, the poor cooped up guys on a ship full of other men for years of their lives. They're the best pilots, all right. And us second-best pilots live a life that the best pilots hunger for.

My amazing guardian angel realized all this in one second, and she decided right away that I must not pass any Navy pilot tests.

Of course she knew that I would never say, Thank You, nor would I know she even existed, and still she worked full-time making everything safe enough that I didn't have to be killed before I wrote the books that I had agreed to write.

All this time she made sure that when I spun an F-86 out of control from night aerobatics, she'd give me enough altitude to recover, she'd make sure that I never had an engine failure, never had to bail out when the controls froze, that I would never hit a mountain in the fog, never had an engine fire. (I had a fire-warning light, but the problem was the warning system, not an unwanted fire in the engine.)

I nearly hit the ground during a gunnery practice mission, but my angel slammed my airplane upward at the last second. I still can't believe it—in one slam, she overstressed my F-86!

I wasn't a crazy pilot, ever, in my flying career. It was the crazy Air Force that did it. I just wanted to visit heaven.

Air Force mechanics had removed the tip tanks from a Lockheed T-33 airplane. The guys had removed those heavy tanks at the wingtips and all that heavy fuel, and left the light little aircraft that remained that day, for me to fly.

Not much fuel, a little over an hour's flight, remained in the main tanks. Not enough fuel to go very far, I thought, but what was different about this day was that I had been given, legally, a light airplane to take up for flying practice.

Just once before, I had flown a clean T-bird, yet that other time there were two of us in the airplane. Today it was just me. What could a light pilot and a clean, light airplane, where could they go today?

It occurred to me and to the airplane in the same second: we couldn't go far, but we could go high! The maximum ceiling printed in the flight manual was 48,000 feet, but no one I knew had come close to that altitude in a T-33.

Forty minutes after takeoff, we had climbed through 39,000 feet, the highest I had ever flown, and the little T-bird was still climbing. As we burned more fuel, she became lighter, and as she was lighter, we could go higher. By the time we had passed 48,000 feet, the T could still climb. Only a few feet per minute, by then, but she was still climbing.

I wondered if we might make it to 50,000 feet, which was very high indeed, at that time. I had switched to 100 percent oxygen in my mask, and was careful to keep the speed less than .8 Mach, its maximum speed. I remembered that the higher you fly, one's limit Mach and one's airplane's stall speed come closer together. Somewhere above us was an altitude when the airplane would stall at the same second she was at her limit Mach. I thought that might be uncomfortable, tumbling end over end, falling uncontrolled into heavier air.

It took us a long time, that day, and we never reached Flight Level 500, as it's now called. The highest we could reach was 49,860 ft. Not one foot more than that would she fly. Our fuel was nearly gone, and for the first time I realized how high we were, how black the sky had become, the curve of the horizon, as though the Earth was a ball and not a flat place at all, and by the way, what a long way down it was to the ground!

I eased the nose down, gently, gently, every move slow and cautious, to keep the engine running in this thin air. If it stopped now, I'd have no jet airplane but a glider till we lost 20,000 feet and then I could hope the T would start again.

Her engine didn't stop. The rest of the flight was easy with so much air around us. I landed with sixty gallons of fuel, taxied to our place on the line and shut the engine down. After I climbed down the ladder to the ground, I thanked her and patted her nose, which was colder than frozen ice.

Until today, I haven't written a word to anyone about what we had done. By now that very T-33A has become a static display on a pedestal near the entry road to some Air Force base, with a secret she never had to tell anyone. On the afternoon of that day, long ago, she had flown higher than any airplane of her kind ever in the world, had flown. I had not found my heaven, but there was no question that she had found hers.

We're fiction to the mortals
who decide to turn left when
we hoped they'd turn right.
Yet we remain friends, and
*they can stay in touch with
us whenever they ask.*
— *The Guardian Angels' Handbook
Volume IX: Working With Your Mortal*

Chapter Two

THIS WAS TRUE. For all my reaching, from an Arizona burro to an F-106B, I never found heaven. And finally, instead of using my body to find this mystical place, I drove my all thoughts and all my beliefs into one green pasture.

From everything I've read, from shelf after shelf of books, from all my intuitions: one idea came forth.

Heaven is a nice place.

Thousands of stories, the research of lifetimes, they all agreed. Heaven is a blissful place: heaven is a beautiful dream that follows our death. *Summerland,* they called it, in the early days. Paradise. There's no death there. The very definition of heaven is that nothing goes wrong in heaven for us, ever.

I agreed with that, and I do, even now. Almost everyone agrees with that. Every context, every subtext means the same: heaven will be joy when we reach that place of mind, whether or not we reach its borders alive, or not-alive. Ask your guardian angel, they said, and she'll confirm that's true.

Listening to this common knowledge, I asked any spirit around me, in my innocence, "Dear spirit, is heaven what they say it is?"

Silence for a minute, then:

"Are you asking me?"

Gentle the voice, not taking place in my mind, but sharing it. I was happy to offer the question to her, since I had no idea who she was.

"Hi," I said. And then, just for fun, I said, "Yes, I was asking you."

I think she may have been startled that at last, after seventy-some years, Richard, her mortal, has finally said a word to her! Asked for an answer. From her, from his own personal guardian angel!

Yes! she thought. I have so much to tell him! But my answer must be true, even when it isn't what he thought it would be.

"Would it be heaven for you," she said, "when your neighbors have parties every day? Would it still be heaven, that way-too-loud sound from their speakers, their dancing going on past midnight?"

What kind of spirit is this? I thought. Yet her question was such an intrigue that I asked again. "No, thank you. No deafening noise, please, no music, no dancing from my neighbors . . . no, thank you. I've had a lifetime of loud noise. Please. That can't be heaven. In hell, yes, that would be fine. But not in heaven, please no."

"So if someone likes music and dance," she said, "you'd send them to hell?"

I smiled for this strange mind in my head, colored with a flash of icy intuition. This was no ordinary spirit who just happened to be there. For me, that never happens. "Oh," I said, testing her. "You must be what . . . a lost soul?"

So confident she was, and so experienced by now, with my mind. "In an empty room," she said, "who else is there to talk with, but me?"

Truth, they say, is that anyone can talk with their guardian angel in an empty room—any spirit, any animal, any extraterrestrial, I guess. Any expression of life can meet us in our quiet mind.

"You've spent a lot of time," I asked, "in heaven?"

"No. Time doesn't exist, in most heavens."

"Let me guess," I said. "No time there, but you've had a lot of experience in heaven."

"Forgive me, but yes, I've had a fair amount of experience with heavens."

"And you're telling me that I could have neighbors like that, soon as I move to heaven?"

"Possible. If . . ."

"If what?"

"If that was your only heaven."

Here's what's fun for mortals:
When they pretend they've
forgotten who they are.

—*The Guardian Angels' Handbook*
Volume IX: Working With Your Mortal

Chapter Three

"My only Heaven," I said.

Since she didn't answer, I improved my question. "My only heaven?"

For all my life, I've believed in one heaven. One heaven for billions of former mortals, and now that I thought about it, maybe millions of extraterrestrials, too. In one heaven? I thought, well, okay. Two heavens. One for mortals, one for ETs.

"Two heavens?" I said, full of sudden questions. "Do we mortals have to sleep near others with high-volume speakers and everybody else dancing past midnight in the dark? Is this my choice? Would you mind, if I move to ET heaven?"

She shrugged. "If that's what you believe . . ."

"I can't believe that! *Heaven is a place for people who love loud noises?*" And then, without even thinking about it, I asked her directly. "One heaven will work for a few discarnates, but for everybody else, it won't be heaven at all, will it?"

I looked to my guardian angel again, and as I did, she looked back at me from the mists of my mind, and put her finger lightly on the tip of her nose.

"That's it?" I said.

She was smiling.

I wasn't. "The spirits who love rap music, the spirits who love classical music, will they both move to the same heaven and how can they live next door to each other?

"The spirits who love city life and the spirits who love country life, the ones who love politics and the ones who can't stand anything political, the spirits who love airplanes and the spirits who wouldn't be caught dead in an airplane—can all these spirits wind up in the same place?

"Will these different people, who have learned these different ways of living, will they meet each other on the streets of heaven, will they spend time with each other in one paradise with neighbors of vastly different values?"

Oh, no, I thought. Are there wars in heaven?

"Thought-forms," she said. "Even Guardian Angel Heaven, it's a thought-form. You want a million miles of undiscovered country to surround you in your own build-it-yourself heaven? Think of it, and it's done! We have whatever we need, in heaven, whatever we want, it's here right now, this minute! If there's one rule in heaven, this is it: *Whatever we desire, it's already ours.*"

Thank God, I thought. No wars. Still, different heavens?

"There have to be different heavens," she said. "People who love war, people who love violence, people who love crime, you'd call it hell, but for them it's heaven, at least for a while."

"Until . . ."

"Until they stop loving it."

All the books I've read about death and dying, filled with stories and accounts and proofs that we go on after this lifetime, how can my heaven be the exactly the same place that it is for everyone who's died in the last thousand years or so?

Is there one place in paradise where some folks enjoy cigars, a different heaven where others travel instantly to other places, others have houses, others don't need shelter from winds or rains, which don't exist in their heaven?

Does heaven require space and time? Can heaven be kind of a dream, where we imagine space and time, but know that space-time doesn't exist?

How many heavens can there be? Two? Twenty? A million heavens, an indefinite number of heavens? Not just for mortals, but for every expression of life and love who recovers from the belief of dying? Do mortals share the same heaven with animals, with bees?

There must be a heaven for dogs and cats who love people, and different heavens for dogs, cats, and other animals who prefer to continue without any humans at all. There must be a heaven for chipmunks and a separate heaven for crocodiles, and different ones for recently arrived spirits who've spent a lifetime thinking that no such place exists.

There must be separate heavens to take care of the people who believe the various religions. Then different heavens for the different ways of thinking.

Separate heavens.

Perfect for those who agree with any one of the countless heavens, countless schools for learning about life and love.

At last my angel shook her head. "Lots of heavens," she said. "And one for you."

A heaven for me. My heaven would need classrooms where I could remember to travel across galaxies in a second or so, visit the past and the future, meet friends from other lifetimes, find how to change appearances from broken into perfection, learn about sharing love (which I have not been too good at, during this lifetime).

"Is your heaven," she said, "the same as the one you're living right now? Is this world a heaven for you?"

"Not by a mile!" I said. "If it weren't for the slowness, if it weren't for the problems with space and time, if it weren't for evil . . ."

". . . for the belief of space and time," she corrected, "for the belief of evil . . ."

"If it weren't for the belief of space-time and evil, and if I could practice these things that I know are true, and if it weren't for material things and all my false beliefs, I think, yes, it would be sort of a heaven, right here."

"And what happens in your sort of heaven, if you believed that you must die?"

"Then I get to choose a different heaven, a place where death doesn't exist."

"And if you decide never to die," she said, "you'll choose a heaven in which you'll never decide to find a different heaven? No one's ever done that.

"Don't you know? What you call 'death' is your chance to make different choices, make different stories about life and love."

"Have you been a mortal? Ever? Long time ago?"

"No," she said. "Too scary for me, too scary for any angel. We never forget who we are. But forgetting who you are, that's something that mortals do every time they turn around. Somehow that's not scary for you, is it?"

How could I tell my angel how many times I've been frightened for just that reason, the times when I've been adrift from any reason to live?

"Just a little scary, once in a while," I said.

"I do I admire you," she said. "You mortals walk into some difficult corners. Your beliefs have corners so sharp that mortals try to kill themselves to escape, and yet you carry these beliefs anyway."

"And the mortals who kill themselves," I said, "they're okay, too?"

"Of course they are. What's suicide? Is that when mortals decide to kill themselves in one second? One second from a fall from high places, one second in their cars? Thousands of mortals do that every year!

"What about suicides that take longer than a second, what about the mortals who die from days or years using drugs or cigarettes or alcohol,—are those suicides, too? How about the mortals who die from a belief of age? Isn't every death a suicide? There's no angel anywhere who'd say one way of dying is okay but a different way is wrong."

"I'm just trying to learn," I said. "I don't know how to make rules."

"No rules is good," she said. "And by the way, that's the way things are. The minute that mortals believe they're dead, they look around and realize they're fine again. And sure enough, before long they may be ready to try mortalship again. They try to do a better job, next time.

"We, your angels, we shake our heads then, but mortals have always been our friends. How could we become guardian angels, if there were no mortals brave enough to forget about reality and sail out there in their illusions of space and time? They build the classrooms in which they'll learn together. You can't help but love these crazy, these brilliant souls."

"Thanks for caring about us," I said.

"Would you mind if I offer," she said, "an idea for your consideration?"

"For my consideration?" I said. "You don't plan on forcing me to do anything? You don't want me to think about anything I don't believe?"

"No."

"Okay. What would you like for me to consider?"

"Would you mind continuing what you're already doing? It's a powerful suggestion. It can help you more in this life than you can imagine."

"That sounds great," I said, and looked around my empty room. "What am I doing?"

Her voice was steady and slower than it had been, as though she didn't want me to be frightened. "What you are doing," she said, slowly, "Is that you are talking with me, your guardian angel."

Then she was quiet for a long time. "And?" I said.

"Thank you," she said, as though she had been holding her breath. "Can I tell you what happens sometimes?"

I was puzzled, but listened. "What happens?" I said, "sometimes?"

"Sometimes the mortals we love, they stop talking. They'll start a conversation from some event they think may be a miracle, and all at once they realize that they're talking with their angel, and then they realize that can't happen unless they've gone mad, so they quit talking.

"They'll ask some lovely questions, in the quiet of their mind, they're in perfect tune with us and all of a sudden they'll stop. It's as if they want the idea of talking with us to be gone, as if they they've just hung up on us. Click. So I thought that you might do the same thing."

"Why would I . . ." and then I thought about what she had said. *Do I really, seriously, think I'm talking in my mind to somebody who doesn't exist?*

Why am I doing this? Am I crazy thinking this, actually having this conversations with, well, with nobody?

That's when our time together stopped.

What will your mortal's life be like without tests, without odds against them, without adventure, without risk? Does the word "graveyard" come to mind?
—*The Guardian Angels' Handbook Volume IX: Working With Your Mortal*

Chapter Four

It was years later, and my plan was excellent. I had thought it through, every part of it, and there wasn't one thing there that would hurt myself or anyone else if they were in my kitchen, which they weren't.

After my solitary dinner of . . . something, I decided to cook up a chocolate pudding. A chocolate pudding with fluffy egg whites mixed together with a little sugar then folded into the warm pudding, would that be good or what?

The plan was an idea. While my wife Sabryna traveled on business, I was alone in our pudding-free kitchen, and no one could stop me from making this idea of a chocolate pudding come true.

I could stop the idea, of course. Yet there was no Great White Shark, as far as I knew, who believed in kitchens, or puddings of any kind. A Great White Shark might believe in me as a tasty dessert, but she knew that I lived in a house on a mountain way above the sea, a never-never land that no shark would accept.

By the time the pudding had begun to boil, I poured the pudding into the fluffed-up egg whites—and there it was: a fluffy chocolate pudding!

I tasted it, found it delicious. Since I was alone, I imagined a person who would talk with me. Someone who designs puddings. Someone who knows more than I do, who enjoys sharing ideas, a person who may not know everything, but who could be miles ahead on the road where I stand.

"Are you here?" I asked, settled at last in my kitchen chair.

A minute of silence. "Don't you know I'm always with you?"

"Always?" I said.

"Always. I've been with you since you were born, I'm with you now, I'll be with you on the day you'll die. It's necessary for guardian angels to be invisible, and since most mortals can't see angels, they rarely believe in us and they hardly ever call."

"Well, how do I unlearn my ability to not-see you?"

"You might try believing in me. Then be patient. You'll gradually begin to imagine me, but you'll need time for this ability to unfold."

"I want it to happen now."

"Didn't I suggest that you can make it happen now? I'm sorry. And the word for you, which will be the same as the word for anyone who sees spirits appearing around them. If you've forgotten, that word is, '*Crazy*.'"

"Oh," I said. "So you're a spirit?"

"In some thoughtless undefined way, I'd say, yes, I am."

"You're a female, aren't you?"

"Yes. That's important for us. How did you know?"

"I just sensed that you are. The way you speak certain words, maybe. Familiar."

"Don't forget. Your sense of who you're talking with, that sense is usually true."

I couldn't help but ask. "Are you beautiful?"

"I'm a spirit!" she said. "I can take any form I wish, and I know what form my mortal would most enjoy. When you live in a space-time world, in the world where you're living right now, I can appear to you as a cat, a dog, an airplane. Haven't you flown some airplanes that you love, and some that you don't care for at all? Don't pilots have some forms, some type of airplanes that they love, too?"

"Well . . ."

"Don't some pilots—I won't name any names—despise, for instance, the North American P-51, yet love other airplanes so much they've owned them, perhaps your little SeaRey, for instance? Seems to me that you love the spirit of that airplane, even when that form was bent, broken pieces on some field? Don't pilots hurt when their airplanes crash, don't they hurt even when one wing gets a little scratch when they've been safe in their hangar?"

"That's possible," I said. "That could be."

"How do mortals feel when their dog dies?" she said. "Some will never recover from the loss of the dear companion spirit who lived with them. If I were to take a space-time form and appeared to you, you can bet you'd think I was beautiful. "

"Oh. And I'm talking now with a spirit."

"Really?" she said. "How many people do you know who talk with spirits?"

"Hmm. I used to know one, but she died."

"So you don't know anyone now who talks with spirits."

"I read about them. They write books, and I read their books."

"Lots of them?"

That's when I found that my angel was playing with me. "Here's the point of my disagreeing," I said. "I'm frightened to become a person who speaks with spirits, even though it's happening a lot, these days."

"Yes. That's happened before."

"It what?" I said. "When?"

"You won't remember. The T-33? Clean, no tiptanks? High altitude? Wasn't Flight Level Five Zero Zero your reaching for heaven? You never told . . ."

"I never told anybody about that!"

"And the next thing you did was to be frightened and then you stopped talking with me," she said. *"The Theory of Many Heavens,* remember that? Now you're frightened again so I guess you'll run away."

Were those tears in her eyes?

"'Bye . . ." she said.

"Don't tell me what to do!" I huffed at her. "Excuse me, but this pudding was my idea and it was also my idea to talk with you, invisible or not, spirit or not! I decide! Now's the time for you to leave, if you'd prefer to do that."

I had not intended to huff at her, but if you listened to that conversation you might hear a small huff, right then.

She dried her tears. "I've never heard of a guardian angel who hung up on her mortal," she said. "That would be a first."

"Well, thank you. And you're a guardian angel?"

"No," she said. "I'm not *a* guardian angel, I'm *your* guardian angel. You're my only client."

"From the day I was born?"

"Nobody's born," she said. "Any birthplace is a mortal actor's marks on the floor for their first scene. Your birthplace is the location where your character steps onstage again. When you're born, that's Act One, Scene One: and the day others say, '*Action!*' It's the moment for you to begin your part in this play."

"And you're my guardian angel, too? Even when I haven't talked with you?"

"Even when you pretend to forget our conversations. This moment we have right now, this little time together is a perk, it happens only once in a while to very few guardian angels."

"Perk?"

"A perquisite."

"Are you a perk for me?"

"Thank you for asking. And yes. It's odd that you ask about perks, for I'm your living perquisite that mortals can find in only one way."

"One way," I said. "And that way is . . . ?"

"By asking," she said.

Every idea is guided by their angels
to the mortal who needs to find it.

—*The Guardian Angels' Handbook*
Volume IX: Working With Your Mortal

Chapter Five

"WHAT AM I supposed to ask?" I said to my empty room.

"Anything you'd care to know," she said.

"That could be anything, I can't think of anything I'd ask, right now."

"Don't think. Just ask."

"Now?"

"Now."

I didn't think, I didn't even open my mouth. Silently I asked my angel what I wanted to know, "How many heavens are there?"

She smiled. "That wasn't hard, was it?"

"No. How many heavens are there?"

"Three," she said. I could tell she was smiling.

"*Three!* Oh, come on! I remember you said . . ."

"Just kidding," she said. "You knew the answer, didn't you? There are . . ."

". . . an indefinite number . . . ?" I said.

"Can you finish your answer?"

I nodded. ". . . of heavens for every expression of life that has ever chosen to live in space-time?"

I knew it was true. No one can count how many . . . I asked another question, one that had puzzled me for years. "When an earthman and a lady extraterrestrial meet and love and marry and die together—which heaven will be their afterlife?"

"You know that answer, too, don't you?" she said.

Instead of "No," I said, "Any one of the millions of heavens that they're invited to enter?"

"And if they don't like the heaven they've chosen?"

"They're not mortals anymore," she said. "They can switch, as spirits often do, to a different heaven."

"Do you know how to show me? Can you take me to different heavens?"

"As a mortal?" she said, "No. But you do have a different sense. I can show you the many heavens in your dreams. You probably won't remember."

"I don't care if I don't remember, I've been thinking about this journey all my life. Every book I've written was about this question. Of course, if you refuse to show me these, even in dreams, that's okay."

"Tell you what," she said. "If you can remember your dreams, I'll take you to every heaven you can imagine."

"Done!" I said.

*Every event in space-time is
some mortal's dream come true.*

—*The Guardian Angels' Handbook
Volume IX: Working With Your Mortal*

Chapter Six

"PERFECT LOVE, perfect Life," she said, "it doesn't dream. Mortals, however, do."

She told me that one of our dreams is that we're separated from Love.

"Bad things happen," she said, "we're poor, we're unloved, we need many things that we don't find in our lives. What do we do when this happens? We assume that infinite Love sees us as broken needy human beings, and we wonder where is our creator, why doesn't She change bad things into good things for us?

"Perfect Love sees us as perfect right now, this second, every instant of our lives. Love knows us as we are, not as the less-than-perfect characters in our dreams. Love doesn't imagine that we're in some conflict with others, that tens or millions of us are killing or being killed in some nightmare war. How can mortals—the perfect expression of perfect love—be harmed? Ever?"

Had she been telling me this, year after year?

"The answer for mortals is that they can fall into a dream, and in their dream they can pretend to be hurt, pretend to be the killers or the killed, if that would be interesting for them. A dream exists for mortals only so long as they sleep.

"When we're partially awake," she said, "the dream changes into better 'lifetimes,' yet never will mortals express your perfect selves until you become perfectly awake."

"That's the question?" I said. "But you're not awake, you're not totally awake, are you?"

"No," she said. "I'm not. I will never be awake, as mortals can be, since I'm part of the dream, myself. I'm the idea of a guardian, the vision of an angel come to help when you call."

I frowned. "But angels are immortal."

She shook her head. "True. Yet we change when mortals' beliefs about angels change.

Once we were tree-spirits, plant devas, fairies, sprites. In some minds and in some lives, angels still live this way." She smiled. "Ten thousand years from now, will you still call me an angel?"

"I don't know," I said. "Right now, *angel* is a good word for you. Well, *guardian* angel. I love the 'guardian' part."

"Ten thousand years from now, you'll still be free to call me an angel, even when no one believes with you."

"I doubt that."

"Why do you doubt that?"

"Because I won't be here, ten thousand years from now."

She laughed. "You're already there, don't you know that? Have you lost all memories of those futures?"

"Do you remember?" I asked.

"Of course I remember. The words were different, but the idea of a guardian angel, of a me with you, that hasn't changed."

"In ten thou . . . in a hundred thousand years, will you and I have met each other . . . well, on the same terms?"

"As mortals? No. That's not my destiny."

"And it isn't my destiny? Ever?"

"You're dreaming many lifetimes. You'll meet many other mortals who seem to be like me. They'll reflect some aspect of my mind, and you'll love them for that. But not me. Have you forgotten so quickly? I have never been mortal! And you'll never be an angel."

"Sorry. But I refuse to accept that."

"A mortal in love with his guardian angel," she said. "May I refuse to accept that, too?"

I was close to saying, 'Can't we pretend?' but I didn't. Instead, I said, "So today I'm writing a story. A fiction story."

"Thank you for pretending," she said. "The ideas you write, those are true. The story? Anything you can imagine."

"You say, 'Mortals are dreaming,' and that's true," I said. "But when I add, 'about their own guardian angel,' though, that's fiction."

She smiled. "'Mortals are dreaming,' that's true. Add 'about their own guardian angels,' that's true for you. It's true for many people. But for others, it's fiction."

"Okay," I said. "It was true for those who believed in guardian angels long before I wrote a word about you. But it's fiction for those who never believed in angels anyway."

She nodded.

A flash of a sudden nightmare.

"Where were you, where was my guardian angel, when my airplane crashed? One second I was ready to land, the next second I was smashed upside down into the ground, pieces of my airplane flying everywhere, fires all around me, I was being killed in a really uncomfortable way, and I really needed some help right th . . ."

"Stop it!" My angel said. *"Listen, Richard!"*

". . . en to maybe stay aliv . . ."

"Listen to me!"

". . . e a little bit long..."

"Please hear me!" she shouted, "I'M YOUR GUARDIAN FUCKING *ANGEL!!*'"

I slammed to a stop in the middle of a word.

"Why can't you understand?" she said, trembling. "There's a reason for every silly stupid thing you do." Her eyes brimmed with tears. "And there's a reason for every brilliant amazing caring thing you do, too! Lucky me, I get to be here not only for your crashes, but to be here for your takeoffs, too.

"Don't you know? Your mission in every one of your lifetimes is to create love, to express love, to treasure love, to paint love in the biggest letters in every color of every language you will ever learn!"

". . . my crash . . ."

"The reason for your crash was for you, for once in this lifetime, to be *helpless!* Can't you see that? All your days you've been in control, your highest right has been for you to learn how to give love. Not one minute was spent learning how to accept the love of others, of your parents, your friends, your lovers, your wife. . ."

"I don't . . ."

". . . and thanks to the crash, your requirement was to live in the love of others, the love of your beautiful wife Sabryna, the love of people you've never met, whose life is love for others. The doctors, the nurses, the strangers who believe in the things you haven't spent one minute believing in. Not the medicine, that matters, but their love for you no matter you're unconscious, no matter you're in some coma, when you're flat on your back in some hospital where . . ."

"I thought . . ."

". . . the reason for your crash is that you needed to be in a hospital, Richard! The only way to get you there, the only way to learn your lesson was to crash little Puff. Your little seaplane, she loved you so much that she destroyed herself for the love of you. And what did you do, when that lesson was over? You . . ."

"I couldn't . . ."

". . . loved her back! You rebuilt her and you flew again together! And you knew that everyone who did their best to keep you alive was sharing their love in ways that you have never seen before. That was the lesson you needed to live, this time around. Can't you understand? Every event in every one of your lifetimes is for you to learn what you need to know . . ."

"And you're my . . ."

"Love! All you need to know in any lifetime is that *Love is the only reality.* Anything else is your dream!"

Silence.

"Is it okay for me to speak?"

She nodded.

"Guardian angels," I said, "they're emotional angels, aren't they? Your language . . ."

"Sorry," she said. "I don't often use explosives. I never use explosives. But the only way I could reach you was with a few words that would make you blink, and *listen* to me!"

"In this world, they're called expletives," I said. Somehow it was important for me to correct what she had said.

"In my world," she said, "they're called explosives. They mean nothing to a mortal who uses expletives all the time, but when you find a mortal who never uses an expletive, then they're explosives, and they can penetrate some pretty heavy armor."

"I neve . . ." I said. "Is that why my mom told me? That the only people who use expletives are the ones who don't have enough intelligence to say an idea in some original way?"

She was quiet for a minute, hearing the silence. Then she nodded, and said, "Yes. That may be why your mom told you, though it isn't quite true. And that's why . . . Don't you know? There are reasons for everything, important reasons for every one of your crashes. I love you! And that love is why I've become your guardian fucking angel!"

She looked at me, her tears dissolving into a guilty smile about her language.

Who can this be? I thought. Why is it that can she be my dear, and for the moment, my guilty guardian angel? Have I been trying to find heaven, while she's simply been loving me, trying to keep me alive?

"There's one other reason for your crash," she said. "The gift. Do you remember that?"

"There was a huge part about the crash that I've forgotten."

"What you've forgotten is a fact for every mortal in the world, and you forgot what it was? It came into your life because you showed that you could tell others, and then you forgot?"

"If I forgot," I said, "then it couldn't have been all that important."

She looked at me astonished, her face still streaked with tears. Then she listened. And in the next minute she became very calm.

"Tell me about the crash," she said, as though she were some sudden lawyer from heaven.

"Did you not see the crash," I scoffed, "when me, your mortal was going to die, when . . ."

"I saw it. But what's important now is for you to tell me about what you saw. What you saw when you died, that can change the lives of a million other mortals."

"One of us is crazy," I said.

"Please do me a favor," she said. "No matter who's crazy, just tell me what you saw."

If for some reason this is important for my angel, I thought, at least I can be kind and do as she asks. "I was on final approach to the field," I said. "Everything looked good. Wheels were down, flaps were down, I was fifty feet in the air, I eased off the power . . ."

"And then what did you do?"

"Nothing. Everything was perfect. We snuggled down to the ground, and I could hear the tops of the grass on . . ."

"Everything was perfect. Even before you snuggled down? Everything was perfect?"

"I'm telling you about the landing that I saw. Do you want what I learned later, about the crash? You wanted to know what I saw, and I'm telling you what I saw. If you want to know about the wires, about the crash, I'll tell you . . ."

"No. Just slow-motion now, what you saw, snuggling down to the ground . . ."

"I was telling you that! Everything was perfect! The wheels were about to touch . . ."

"That instant, when everything was perfect," she said, "that was when the wires caught Puff's wheels and she crashed inverted into the ground! How could it be perfect that second when you crashed? The crash was a perfect time in your life?"

"I don't care about the crash! I'm telling you what I saw! I didn't see any wires, I didn't feel any crash, it was going to be a beautiful landing!"

"But to the mortals who happened to watch your landing . . ."

"Well, of course! They saw the crash!"

"But you didn't!"

"I didn't know about the crash till a week later, when I came out of the coma. But you wanted to know what I saw at the time of the crash, and I'm telling you what I saw."

"You saw no crash?" she asked, "no pain, no destroying of your body, no destroying of your airplane, no fires . . ."

"Nothing of that," I said. "Just a perfect landing, the wheels about to touch . . ."

"And then?"

"You know what I saw. I was in the air again. Floating in the air in some strange vehicle, some flying-saucer-like machine: no wings, no engine, no crew."

"And then what?"

"Why are you asking? You know 'then what.'"

"Stay with me, please. There's a reason I want you to say then what."

"Then I heard someone say what they said."

"Which was . . ."

" 'Do you want to return to your life on Earth?'"

"Thank you."

"Thank me for what?"

"For saying that you had a choice. You could have chosen to leave your life on Earth or you could have stayed. That rarely happens."

"Seemed normal to me."

"Yes!" she said, as if I were brilliant again. "Yes! We have the power of vanishment of our beliefs, in this world as well as in heaven.

"Mortals in extreme violence, mortals in a crash like yours, they're the same," she said.

"You use your skills at vanishment to erase parts of your dream. You aren't aware of any crash, any violence. All at once you're in a different dream, you arrive at the gates of your heavens. Most other mortals' time on earth is over, their choice has already been made."

It was quiet for a while. "And that's your gift," she said.

"The crash was a gift." I said that, but I didn't believe it.

"How many mortals have that experience, have the chance to tell others that nobody dies? How many wives," she said, "how many children, how many survivors of violence, the ones who remained on Earth after their mortal friends were killed, might like to know what you know, right now?

"Wouldn't they like to know that their loved one didn't see any explosion, any fire, but instead they dreamed their way gently into their own heaven? That the ones they loved are perfect right now, this instant, and they'll be meeting them again, before long? What would you call that? Would you call that a terrible truth? Or would you consider the lesson from your crash to be a gift to mortals?"

They say that when our angels suggest a lesson for us, and we don't understand what it means, that they'll give us the same lesson . . . over and over, until we understand.

Could that be true? I believe now that the events that happened after my crash have been a gift for anyone who loves to fly, and to the ones who love them.

No expectations, no failure.
Your mortal can't tell whether
that's an easy life or not.
—*The Guardian Angels' Handbook*
Volume IX: Working With Your Mortal

Chapter Seven

IT WAS DAYBREAK, and sort of remembering, I opened my eyes. "Guardian angels do a lot of waiting, don't they?"

"It's part of our work," she said. "Do you know any impatient angels?"

"Guilty angels, yes," I said. "Impatient angels? I can't name one."

"I was not guilty! I may have seemed that way to you, but I wasn't. Sometimes we need to say whatever's necessary to reach our mortal."

"I understand," I said. "Do you need to do certain things, sometimes, too? Not words, but actions?"

"Rarely. Almost never. Strong words, now and then. Actions, no."

"Hmm."

"What does 'hmm' mean?" she asked. "Why are you looking puzzled?"

"I guess you weren't there."

"I'll doubt that. I've been with you since you were born. Remember the burro? I didn't do anything with Pete. I talked to him and he listened."

"The AT range," I said. "In gunnery school. The day my F-86 nearly hit the target."

"Words again. *The hand of God.* Those words seemed to be enough for you."

"No. A few seconds before that. When I knew I had gone too low, and my airplane itself was going to hit directly into the center of my target. Remember that? Cold morning, in the desert. No thermals, no updrafts. And before I hit . . . Do you remember that?"

"I've asked you to forget that."

"Well, I didn't."

She said nothing.

"It's been fifty years, now, and I've remembered. There was no way I could have missed crashing into that target, we were milliseconds from becoming a fireball in the desert. And somehow . . ."

Quiet.

". . . somehow my airplane, before I could even move the control stick . . . I was in a steep dive, remember? But all of a sudden, the airplane was slammed upward, blacked me out with the force of those G's. Two seconds later I could start to see again, and found we were a thousand feet in the air! A thousand feet! Not possible. No way in . . . heaven . . . this airplane could be flying again! No way. Not possible."

Not a word from my guardian angel.

"Why, dear angel? That's the only mystery left in my mind, after all these years. Why didn't I die that morning?"

She muttered something.

"Excuse me? I didn't hear what you said."

"Exceptions," she whispered.

"Exceptions? Tell me."

"No."

"That split second was an exception," I said. "It was different from every other second in my life!"

"Yes," she said, and brightened. "Would you like some chocolate ice cream? There's nearly a whole pint of ice cream, right now, in your freezer!"

"You made that happen, didn't you?"

"Just a little bit. You know how good that ice cream is? I don't think I've ever seen such a delicious pint almost, of ice cream!"

"I've never forgotten that moment," I said. "It overstressed . . . *even the F-86 was overstessed!* Limit G in that airplane was 7G. That time, some force slammed the '86 upward, it was 8.7G on the recording G-meter right there on the instrument panel in that very cockpit!

"Later I calculated. To pull those G's, on that airplane, it needed 161,000 pounds of lift to recover my airplane from a dive at 350 knots. And that was what everybody else would have called an 'updraft.' A 'lucky updraft?' A lucky eighty-one tons of lift from an altitude of five feet over an ice-cold desert? That is not the truth, dear angel."

Quiet.

"Can you please do me a favor?" I asked. "Please tell me the truth. I promise that I will never stop asking about it, no stopping from asking, no ice cream, no nothing but please tell me what happened that day!"

She sighed. "It's a long story," she said. "How about some absolutely delicious ice cream, instead?"

"No, thank you. Maybe later about the ice cream. Not now."

She sighed again. "The best I can say is that every guardian angel is allowed one miracle, to use for special-case events. Usually, when our mortals make a silly mistake, that's their destiny, it's the end of their lifetime, and they'll 'die' and we can escort them home to their heaven. We can chat later about why they did such a thing. Of course there's a reason for it, which they'll discover for themselves."

"That's reasonable," I said. "Now. About my destiny at the Applied Tactics range . . ."

"Once in a . . ." she said, "once in a long while, there are exceptions."

"Tell me about exce . . ."

"No. We've agreed, you and me, never to tell you about exceptions while you're a mortal. Let's just say that possibly, and perhaps with my request, there happened to be an extremely powerful thermal, a vertical current of air that formed at an altitude of five feet above the desert, which was destined to meet your airplane at exactly the instant when eighty-one tons of lift was required to throw you and your F-86 a thousand feet into the sky."

She didn't smile. "That's my story, and I'm sticking with it."

"The reason I've been hoping to find, after all these years," I looked at her, "is that you cashed out your one miracle for your mortal, in order to save his life?"

After a silence, she finally found some words. "I can neither confirm nor deny the experience that you remember, no matter what may or may not have happened at the AT range."

An event that occurred fifty-some years ago. It took that long, and my reluctant guardian angel, to tell me why it happened.

What does "recursive" mean,
and why is your mortal
trapped in this hall of mirrors?
—*The Guardian Angels' Handbook*
Volume IX: Working With Your Mortal

Chapter Eight

"I GUESS YOU'RE RIGHT," I said into the empty air of my midnight kitchen. "It was an exception when I didn't die when I should have done just that."

I wondered if she was still listening.

"I'm here," she said, barely audible.

I smiled. "You're always here, aren't you?"

"Time," she said. "That's part of your world."

"Maybe. It's just that whenever I ask for you, you're always here. As if you do nothing but lounge around on some pillow, eating bon-bons, until your phone rings."

"My time is different from yours. I have other things to do, meetings, classes, planning events in your future," she said. "Care for a bon-bon?"

"What if I said, 'Yes. Hand me a bon-bon, please.' What would you do then?"

"I'd offer it to you, of course. Where did all that chocolate pudding come from?" she said. "I'm always here for you in your time. At the same time . . . well in a different time, some would say that I'm a busy angel."

"Are there any lazy angels?"

"No."

"A lazy angel is no angel," I said.

She laughed. "She's a mortal."

"Let's keep things straight between us," she said. "I'm an angel, I'm your messenger. When there are important ideas to be carried, angels are the messengers, and our mortals are the messengees."

Before I could answer, she continued. "Don't forget: You're my mortal! You cause events to happen, and once in a while you wonder why they happened as they did. I'll help you along your path, and sometimes, and only when you ask, I can tell you why. Still, you decide the events that will change both of our lives." She touched her breast. "I'm the messenger. You're the one who decides whether or not you'll listen to your angel."

"Sometimes," I asked, "do you think that mortals don't listen to our angels?"

"Yes," she said. "I believe that may have happened."

Angels, I thought, do they appear with their own sense of humor?

"The word you use for yourselves—*mortal*—" she said, "do you know it comes from Latin, the word *mort*, which means—listen to this: *death!* Are you mortals the dead people?

"We angels are defined by your same old Latin dictionary as *spiritus, breath, SPIRITS*, for God's sake! Are mortals nothing but vampires? Are you the dead trying to live again?

"Don't you think it would be well for mortals to listen to, at least to their guardian angels who for some reason they can't explain, *love their mortals?*"

I listened, and I wondered how she can be a messenger, yet still be my guardian angel.

"Who do you think I was," she said, "when that lucky updraft kept you from becoming a fireball at the AT range?

"Where do you think I was when you heard the words *Jonathan Livingston Seagull*?

"When your parachute failed, who reminded you, quickly, I might add, *Pull the reserve!*

"Who did you hear when somebody said, *Start your pullout early!* and you missed touching a German tank with the nose of your F-84 at the speed of three hundred fifty some knots?

"Who mentioned, *Move to the right!* before you got out of the way of another airplane landing the opposite way on that runway?

"Where was I, when somebody asked if you might wish to return to your life on earth, after your most recent crash?

"Who was the messenger those days, and who might have been, could have been, probably was, your own private, personal guardian angel? Did you think that she was some transient angel, some angel on her way to the grocery store?"

It was my turn to be quiet.

*The world of space, time and
appearances can be wondrous beautiful.
Have care, though, and don't let
your mortal mistake them for real.*
—*The Guardian Angels' Handbook
Volume IX: Working With Your Mortal*

Chapter Nine

"I WANT TO SEE some heavens."

"No," said my guardian angel. "That's not a good idea."

"Not a good idea? You're the very one, you're the angel who told me that there are lots more heavens than one, and now you've what—changed your mind?"

"Do you know how many heavens there are?" she said. "Every one of them: a custom-made afterworld. Built to be perfect for anyone who's qualified to enter there. Some heavens have streets and scenes from the 1890's; everything from that time is perfect for a few former mortals. Others heavens have twenty dimensions. Some have no animals, others have only animals. All these heavens, each one different from every other heaven."

"Qualified former mortals?" I said. "Qualified?"

"Mm-hmm," she said with a nod. "Former mortals are qualified by the beliefs they entertain. When any mortal believes in evil, for instance, they aren't qualified to enter any heaven, even a friend's heaven, in which no evil is allowed."

"You said you'd show me. You said heavens would be learning experiences for me."

"As long as you're currently a mortal, that's true. Heavens are merely beliefs for you, they're dreams."

"So I can go with you to anybody's heaven."

"Technically, that's true."

"But . . . ?"

"Would you care to visit a murderer's heaven? *'Hi, Jack the Ripper, Richard wants to visit your perfect place. Would you mind if he looks around this heaven for a while?'"*

"Stop! Not a murderer's heaven. You're right. Not a Bonnie and Clyde heaven, either."

"How about a heaven from those with different cultures?" she said. "Would you enjoy your visit when everyone there speaks Swedish, or Japanese, or Tibetan?"

"Okay, we can cross those off."

"How about the heavens from different times," she said. "Are you happy to visit the heavens from ancient Greece, from . . ."

"Will they speak Greek?"

"Attic Greek, yes."

"We can let those go."

"How about the heavens of people who lived in 18th century England? Interested in those? They're in English . . ."

"No."

"A nun's heaven?"

"No."

"A politician's heaven?"

"No."

"A seal-hunter's heaven?"

"Grf. No!"

"Perhaps you can simply list the heavens you would prefer to visit."

You win, I thought. "I'd like to visit my heaven. That's plenty. Just mine."

"Your heaven? That's still under construction. Just pieces, not connected yet."

"Everybody's gets their own heaven and I don't?"

"You're a mortal!" she said. "Your heaven won't be finished until the day you die."

"What needs to be finished? I could die tonight!"

"But you're still learning," she said. "You used to believe that things happened by chance. Now you don't.

"You used to believe that you had never met your parents, your family, your lovers, your wives, your friends, your enemies, before the time you met them here on earth. You don't believe that, now.

"Do you want your afterlife to continue on old beliefs? Do you believe that evil should continue there?

"You once believed that death was a kind of blackness. Do you prefer to continue that ancient belief into your heaven yet to come?"

"The more I learn," I said, "the more will I change and love my heaven. Is that true?"

"Do you need me to confirm that to you? What if I said, *No, that's not true at all.* What would you say to me, if I said that?"

"I'd suggest that you were still in Guardian Angel training."

"Then I'll leave the question of your truth for you to decide."

"Thank you," I said. We were quiet for a long time. "Am I in your heaven?" I said, at last. "Are you in mine?"

"You know the answer," she said. "I come from a heaven where all angels live. Our heaven is beyond . . . well, it's different from mortals' heavens."

"And you commute to your business on earth."

She laughed. "No need to commute. You're my business on earth, 36/10. I'm always with you."

"24/7."

"36/10, Angel Time."

My angel wanted to finish the subject of heavens, finish it forever. "Tell me the name of a friend," she said. "Tell me about someone you've known, and liked, any friend whom you would now consider to be dead."

"Any friend?"

"Anybody dead, yes."

"From a long time ago, or recently just died?"

"Doesn't matter. Any friend."

I hadn't thought of him for years, but suddenly there he was in my mind. Gene Dexter had been an F-105 pilot, shot down by ground fire during the war in Viet Nam. I knew him when we were roommates in pilot training. He liked alcohol, but nearly every pilot did, then. He played the guitar, taught me a few songs that to this day I still remember.

"Gene Dexter."

"Oh," she said. When she had asked about a dead friend, I forgot that my guardian angel already knew about Gene, she was there with me when we had met.

"Do you mind if I ask?" she said.

"Certainly. Ask away."

"Can you imagine a heaven for Gene that does not have what he believes to be alcohol?"

"Alcohol? In heaven?"

"A belief of alcohol. In his own personal heaven."

"You mean we'd say Hi, and then he'd bring some glasses and pour . . ."

"Do you think he wouldn't be kind to you, his old friend, set you up with a drink and then begin to relive the times you've shared, the lessons you've learned? The time he was required to wear that necklace from a T-33 tiptank cap, because he forgot . . ."

"He didn't laugh that day."

"He would now. So that would be fun, to meet him again?"

"Of course! We were roommates!"

"And you'd love to see him again, drunk or not. He'd laugh about the times you told him it was crazy for him to carry on drunk like that?"

"No. He wouldn't laugh."

"If he did, you'd just stomp out of his own heaven?"

"I wouldn't stomp! I'd close the door quietly behind me."

"Because Gene's heaven would be hell for you," she said.

"I guess, after a while, maybe a little."

"And he'd enjoy remembering when you woke him from his sleep after you read something in the T-33 Dash-One that you thought he needed to know about?"

"He didn't prefer waking to hear what I found for him at the time, no."

"Do you think there's a reason why you may not enjoy visiting his heaven, or any heaven but your own?"

"I'd just stay for a little while."

"Because if you stayed longer, you'd beg to be taken away from there?"

"I don't think I'd want to live Gene's heaven, no."

"And he wouldn't want to live in yours?"

"I guess not. A life without parties for Gene? That would be hell for him."

"Do you need to experience that for your-self? Or can you imagine," she said. "Wouldn't anybody's heaven have problems for you?"

"Some wouldn't. Well, probably. Yes." I thought for a second or two. "It could be that I'd go crazy in their heaven. They'd love mine, of course, since everything will be in perfect order, there. Are you saying, dear angel, that people in heaven don't live together?"

"The bond between people," she said, "is . . . ?"

"Love, of course."

". . . Love," she said. "When heaven-people want to see others, when it's a delight for them, when they enjoy being together, they do that. When they love events that cross many heavens, they can meet there. And some private events, too. But live with each other, all the time? It's possible, with the billions of heavens that exist, but that's a little on the rare side."

"And there are many different sides to time," I said, feeling as though I was in training for her job, "But the truth is that heaven's a lonely place."

"If you want to be alone," she said. "When you love your quiet times, are you lonely?"

Never, I thought. "Not when I have my own beautiful personal guardian angel to teach me whatever I need to know. And every mortal has a guardian angel. I've heard that. True?"

"Of course that's true," she said. "And with every step you take in this space-time world, you're earning your next heaven. Your own heaven is not some impossible puzzle, it's your own private belief of heaven.

"You can work right now, today, as a mortal, to refine your beliefs, to make your heaven happier than the squirrelly heaven you've already built with your not-much-thought-about belief system. You can do this now."

"And let me guess," I said. "All guardian angels are just as beautiful as you are, and they're just as smart as you are."

She frowned. "We're all beautiful, we're all smart, but don't forget: *we're messengers!* How many mortals do you know who would want to spend their life listening to messages from a thoughtless trashed-out troll-spirit?"

I had to smile at her frown. "If there's one poor mortal who would prefer that, there's probably one trashed-out troll-spirit willing to apply for the position."

"It's kind of you to suggest that. The meaning of the word *beautiful* can change, from one mortal to another, but in the heart of any soul, beauty cannot vanish, and there's no power that can make it disappear. I'm beautiful *to you*. Maybe not beautiful for other mortals, but to you, I am."

"Other mortals don't believe in angels," I said. "Because you're invisible! We can't see you, they say, so therefore, you can't exist."

She shrugged. "Is that what they say?"

"You know that's true."

"Aerodynamics: that's invisible, too. Do you know any pilots who refuse to believe in aerodynamics?"

If I stopped believing in aerodynamics, I thought, I'd never have become a flyer. Even angels had to believe in at least spiritual aerodynamics, or they couldn't fly. If they believed they're not required to make our lifetimes into learning experiences, there's no purpose for us in their lives. And no purpose for angels in our lives, either.

"Love," she said. "Is love visible? What would our lives become if we refuse to allow love? When love is required for your lessons, we can become very sexy angels."

"Sexy angels?" I said, with a smile. "Oh, come on."

"If I dared to become even half, even one-quarter as sexy as any angel can be, I promise that you'd believe in angels forever!"

"You," I said, unconvinced, "you're beautiful, but can you be sexy? Somehow 'angel' and 'sexy' are two words that don't quite . . ."

"Oh, you don't believe me? Would you like me to slip into my off-the-shoulder robe, the one with the scarlet sash? Give me a second . . ." In half that second she was half-undressed.

"Wait!" I said, "Wait! I believe you! I believe you!"

There was a moment of silence. Then she adjusted her robe up to the place it ought to be.

"Thank you for believing in me," she said at last. "My job is to guide you on the path to your heaven. I doubt that my guidance was required to follow that particular path."

*In those rare moments when mortals know
they're one with Love, are they One just for that
moment, or have they been One forever?*

—*The Guardian Angels' Handbook
Volume IX: Working With Your Mortal*

Chapter Ten

SHE'LL BE WITH me till the end of my life.

When I asked, she said she'll stand near me for my end-of-life review with the most experienced spirits.

"But what?" she said.

"But will you be with me when I meet the ones who were my parents, my friends, my dogs and cats on the other side? Will you be there when I move into my own heaven? If ever I try another lifetime, will you be with me then?"

"You've asked for me to be with you for this life, and you're the only one who can extend my contract. You know that in your next lifetime you'll forget about contracts, you'll forget about angels, you know that, don't you? Do you want me to stay, and be your Forgotten Angel, yet again?"

All that was required to meet our guardian angel was simply to ask, simply to say Hi to our invisible friend, ask any question, and listen to her answer. "I'll remember to ask, next time," I said, "and I'll do that a whole lot earlier than I did this time."

"As long as I haven't brought you back with burro-prints on what was left of your body, the senior angels, they'd probably agree it was okay to continue with our little adventure."

"As I'm sure you know," I said, "I'm burro-print free. You'll be graduating when I finish this lifetime, you'll be an experienced, you'll be a Professional Guardian Angel! Are you sure you'd want to go on with me, instead of guiding someone else? If you like my style, you could try herding cats, next time!"

"They keep trying," she said, "the dear angel cat-herders. They just need to have enough time."

"The cat-herders, are they human-like angels?"

"Don't be silly. Human-like angels don't have nearly enough patience for that job. Cat-angels are working on that. They've been trying that job for thousands of years."

"Are there duck-angels, too?"

"Of course. They solved that problem a long time ago."

"And the horse . . ."

"Horse-angels have no problem herding horses, anytime, anyplace."

"Do human-angels work with horses, too?"

"Some do. We give our hearts to horses, dogs, ducks . . . to any life-form that we love. If you had a pair of spirit-goggles, you could watch all kinds of angels working with all kinds of mortal life-forms."

"Are there ant-angels, too?"

"I've never met an ant-angel. There's quite a different psychology for ants, they say, a group psychology. I hear there's not a strong individual sense there. Bees, they say, there's a hive mentality. Supposed to be one for ants, too. I don't know. I'm not much of an expert on ant problems."

"Angel problems?"

"Such as there are. Not many angel problems."

"Would you say that there are possibly five angels with problems? Seven?"

"I'd say there are possibly zero angels' problems. Approximately zero."

"Because you're immortal. Is that why?"

"We're immortal and we know it. Humans are immortal and they don't know it. They mix physical mortality, which lasts for about two seconds, with spiritual immortality which lasts forever. Cows can understand that, mortals can't."

*Runes and tarot, yarrow sticks
and stars in their constellations,
they're psychic placebos.
They give your mortal permission
to remember what they already know.*
—*The Guardian Angels' Handbook
Volume IX: Working With Your Mortal*

Chapter Eleven

"WHEN YOUR MOTHER died . . ."

"My mother didn't die," I said. "You know that. My mom decided to set off on a voyage to a different land."

"The same voyage that dying people set off on?"

"Sort of like that, yes," I said.

"When mortals decide to cross an ocean," she said, "they don't expect to see each other in person, for a while. Why do mortals grieve when their mother, when any loved person, moves to a different land? Do they think that grieving is somehow required? What's the difference between their travels on this planet, and their travels through the different countries of forever?"

"Well . . ."

"You said it, Richard: 'We're connected by the bonds of love that we've built.' With anyone. With our parents, with our friends, with our pets, with fictional characters from books or motion pictures, with characters in our own imagination! Don't you see? The only true bonding happens through strands of love.'"

"I didn't say that."

"All right," she said, "you didn't say that. Do you believe that's true?"

"Yes."

"So you . . ." she said, "so nobody is required to grieve when a loved person travels to a new country."

Maybe, I thought. But it's been difficult, though, not-grieving, when someone close to me decides to leave.

"Mortals are free to grieve," she said, "if that makes them feel better, but it isn't required. You know from the lesson of your own crash, that dying is a beautiful experience. When you grieve over a loved one's dying, when your tears about their joy make you happy, then I think there could be something wrong with your attitude."

"You're such an honest angel! I can't think of one mortal who'd agree with you about not-grieving. But you suggest it, anyway."

She couldn't tell if that was a compliment of not. "Would you disagree?"

"No. I think you're right about that."

"Will you remember me, when I'm gone?" she said, "will you value my reputation as your honest guardian angel?"

"Gone? Your reputation?"

"I may be a new Guardian Angel, but I do have a reputation to think about. Mortals spend a lifetime building their reputation. Angels do that, too. My life with you will dissolve when you die, but as long as histories are written, our mortal's reputation will be remembered. I don't care much about pride, but I'm glad we shared this lifetime together."

"Your life won't dissolve!" I said. "I'll write about you, about your reputation. I'll write about the way you saved me from explosions and fires and motorcycles and burros. I'll write about the way you traded your one miracle to save my life. I'll write about the terrible language you used on me when I was helples . . ."

"When you were attacking me! When you didn't know a thing about the important . . . about the reasons for your crash!"

"If you thought I was attacking you," I said, "then I'm sorry. I didn't mean to attack you, and I won't write about your terrible language."

"Thank you," she said. "It would be kind of you, to leave that out."

"You're welcome." I said, "I'll leave it out, unless it's important, which it probably won't be, but it might be . . ."

"If somehow I find my spirit goggles, then there'd be no question about the existence of my angel, no reader would blink about your many versions of heaven."

"Probably not," she said. "The goggles haven't been invented, remember?"

"But if the goggles were in some different form, couldn't we see our angels and our heavens, now, instead of waiting until we die?"

"Yes," she said. "The form, the invention of those goggles doesn't matter. The fact of angels and heavens is all around us, but since we're mostly invisible, mortals are blind to us."

"How did I learn to see my guardian angel," I asked, "when I was blind to every invisible truth?"

A quiet minute. "You'll have to tell me."

"I don't need the goggles. It's you my dear angel! You can show me, you can show mortals the sweep and the colors and the life of our own heavens, our own Summerland. Is it a secret for us, the way to bring your truth, your vision into our minds?"

"There's no secret," she said. "Didn't I tell you? Mortals need only turn to their angels, and ask. Next thing you know, we answer!"

"No! No! Have you forgotten? I'm a mortal, now. I need to have physical proof before I believe in any angel! I need to hold something, hold something physical and . . ."

"Soft?"

". . . something physical and soft and . . ."

"Feathery?"

". . . soft and feathery . . ."

". . . soft and feathery that will connect me directly to you . . ."

"Who happens to be invisible," she said.

". . . directly to you, and to every angel who happens to be invisible for us mortals."

Silence. "I wish I could help you, Richard. What you think you need may not be your mission in this lifetime."

"I need this . . . this *something!* Could it be a sub-mission for me? There's got to be some way to make this happen! Some magical connection, to remind us mortals that you're always with us, even when we can't see you."

Silence. "Are you in a hurry?"

"Sort of. Why do you ask?"

"It's taking care of itself," she said.

"And I don't need to ask about it, even ask about what it may be?"

"No."

Chapter Twelve

EVER SINCE I'VE DISCOVERED how to open a conversation with my guardian angel, she just goes on about starting our projects by herself, and she doesn't much care about what I think we should do.

It isn't that I have a bossy guardian angel, she simply knows me enough, and now I trust her enough, that good things begin without me worrying about how to make them happen.

That's why I've written these things. I write because at last I know that our angels will answer, when we ask. If you've been taking your time about meeting with your guardian angel, or worried that you might seem a little odd when you chat with her in that empty room . . . why, that's normal!

I guess there must be thousands of us who don't care what others may think about us. Angels aren't an empty wish, or fading images from an old dream.

When I ask, she answers.

Invisible though she may be, my guardian angel has always been with me. She has swept monsters from my path, saved me from wild burros, she's lifted me from the craters of my own mistakes.

I'm free to talk with my guardian angel now, or I can wait until my life is falling apart, and try it then. Either way, it seems to work.

RICHARD BACH is the author of twenty-five books, including *Jonathan Livingston Seagull*, *Illusions*, and *The Bridge Across Forever*. His books have sold tens of millions in over 40 languages throughout the world. Back to back, his work has been on the *New York Times* bestseller lists for more than four years. He deals, most simply and effectively, with ideas that have the power to change the world.

Rainbow Ridge Books publishes spiritual and
metaphysical titles, and is distributed by Square One
Publishers in Garden City Park, New York.

To contact authors and editors, peruse our titles, and
see submission guidelines, please visit our website at
www.rainbowridgebooks.com

For orders and catalogs, please call toll- free:
(877) 900-BOOK

Related Titles

If you enjoyed *Life with My Guardian Angel,*
you may also be pleased to know that
Richard Bach's classic,

Messiah's Handbook

is back in print and now available.

Thank Your Wicked Parents is also
published by Rainbow Ridge Books.